DRAWING
MANGA
STEP-BY-STEP

DRAWING
MANGA
STEP-BY-STEP

BEN KREFTA

ARCTURUS

ARCTURUS

This edition published in 2013 by Arcturus Publishing Limited
26/27 Bickels Yard, 151–153 Bermondsey Street,
London SE1 3HA

ISBN: 978-1-84858-863-9
CH000710US
Supplier 13, Date 0813, Print run 2091
Author & Illustrator: Ben Krefta
Design: Steve Flight

Printed in China

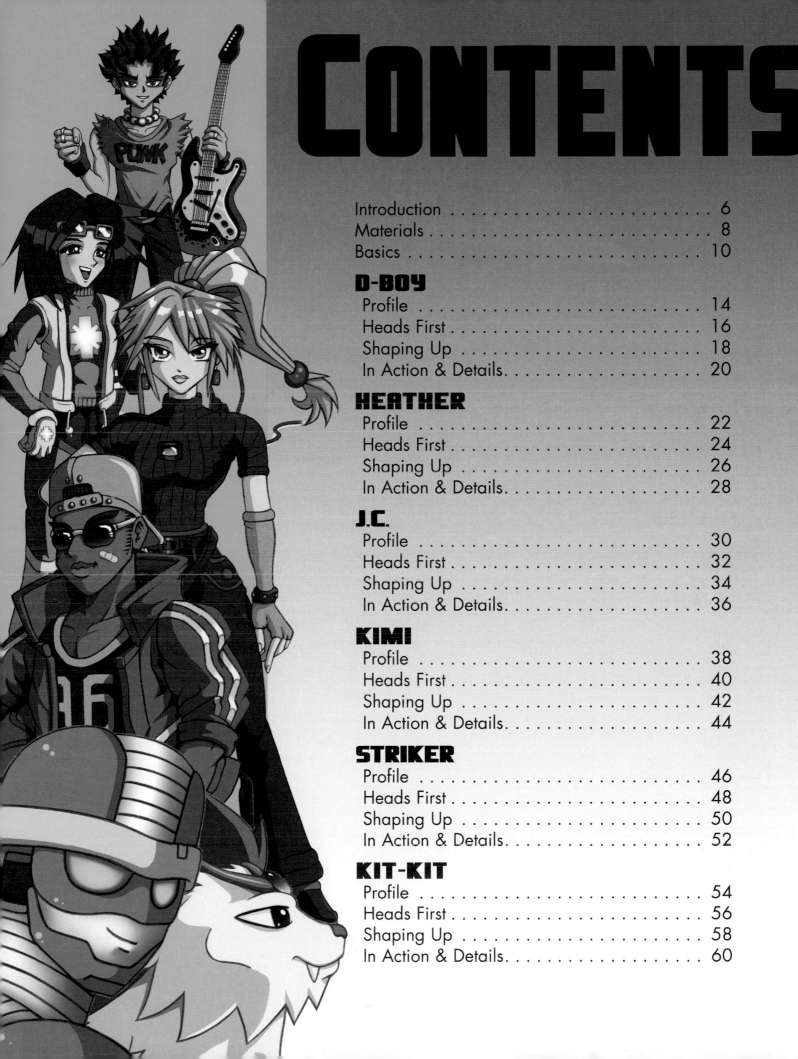

CONTENTS

INTRODUCTION

Welcome to manga, where wide-eyed youngsters collide with mean, muscular monsters—a world where anything is possible. A world that has taken our world by storm.

Created over 50 years ago in Japan, manga literally translates as 'irresponsible pictures,' and is a Japanese art form for comic books. Although early Japanese animation (anime) was influenced by American cartoons of the time, manga stories tend to concentrate on people, not superheroes. Manga art tends to rely on simple, smooth line-art rather than heavy shading like typical cartoons. And while the characters often appear simplistic, there is an emphasis on detail that can be pretty awesome.

We have created six new manga characters for you to learn to draw. Meet D-Boy, the hottest shot on the basketball court; Heather, a girl you would not want to mess with; aspiring rock star J.C.; and Kimi, ice-cool queen of the snowboard. There's Kit-Kit, who's so hot he's smokin', and Striker, a robot who is definitely not the mean, lean fighting machine he was meant to be.

We show you how to draw each character, from matchstick figure to finished, full-action, full-color pose. We also tell you what materials to use and how to use them. So let's get drawing, manga-style.

D-BOY

HEATHER

J.C.

KIMI

STRIKER

KIT-KIT

MATERIALS

What do I need to draw manga? How many pencils will I need to make the first rough sketch? What kind of pen is right for inking-in the draft drawings? And do I use paints or markers to add further color? Is it all going to cost a fortune? RELAX! You've probably got most of what you need lying around the house, and what extras you do need to get started can be bought at any art store, maybe even at your local supermarket. Getting started is quick and simple—all you need is imagination.

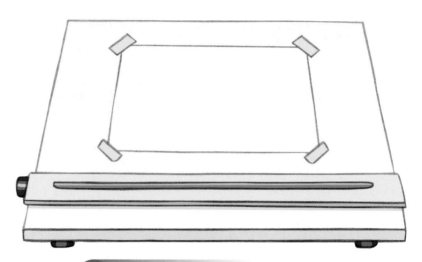

↑ Drawing board

If you draw a lot, as I do, you need to be comfortable. An angled board allows you to secure your paper and stop it getting creased or torn. It also helps you to make perfect straight lines, which you'll need when laying out comic strip panels.

↑ Lead pencils

The 'lead' in a pencil is actually a type of carbon called graphite. It's mixed with clay and fired in an oven. The more clay in the 'lead' the paler the line. Pencils are graded: 1H through to 6H, HB,1B through to 6B, from hardest to softest. I use three—1H, 2H, and 3H, but mostly the 2H. Use the one that works best for you.

↑ Mechanical (technical) pencil

Use one of these for fine draft work. They never need sharpening. The lead comes in various grades from 6H to 6B and can be bought separately. They come in all sorts of shapes and sizes. Find one that's right for your grip.

↑ Black fine line pen

These pens are graded 01 to 05 according to the width of the line they draw. Use the lowest grade for inking fine outlines.

↑ Nib pen

When you're happy with a draft drawing, you can use a nib pen to ink it in. The greater the pressure you put on it, the thicker the line you'll get. Different nibs give different line sizes. The nibs come oiled to prevent rusting, so you have to wipe new ones before you use them.

↑ Paint brush

Use a medium or fine-tip brush for painting in acrylic or watercolor.

⬆ Marker

This is great for color work; it's easier to use than paint and a brush and safer, too! There's no ink or paint to spill when coloring your work and accidents do happen.

⬅ Black India ink

Ink is either water-soluble, which can be diluted with water to make it easier to use; or water-resistant, which doesn't tarnish. Take your pick. If you're using water-soluble ink, it's very important that you wipe the pen nib when you've finished to prevent rusting.

⬆ Eraser

Use a solid eraser for rubbing out draft pencil marks.

⬅ ⬇ Ruler and pencil sharpener

No prizes for guessing what these are for! Try to find a beveled-edge ruler. Less smudging!

⬆ Putty eraser

Because they don't shed tiny bits on the paper, putty erasers are cleaner to use than ordinary erasers.

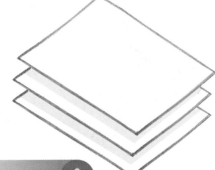

Paper ⬆

You can spend a fortune on drawing paper, but you don't need to. I use quality printer paper, almost like card. It's very smooth (perfect for drawing), very white, and cheap, too.

⬆ Brush pen

Use one of these for especially thin black lines and for filling in blocks of color. It's best to use one for black and a separate one for color work.

BASICS

Our bodies are built around our bones—round ones, curved ones, and straight ones. Attached to the bones are the muscles that give our bodies shape—and there are more shapes in our bodies than in a geometry book.

Getting the proportions of your manga figures right is important. If your proportions are off, your figures won't look real. Using the head as the main unit of measurement, try to stick to the following guide:

- Measuring from head to toe, the head should go into the figure about 7 to 8 times.
- From top of head to shoulders: about 1½ heads; the shoulders should be about 2 heads wide.
- From top of head to hips: about 3 heads down; in men the hips should be narrower than the shoulders (about 1½ wide), and in women about the same (about 2 heads wide).
- From top of head to knees: about 5 heads down.

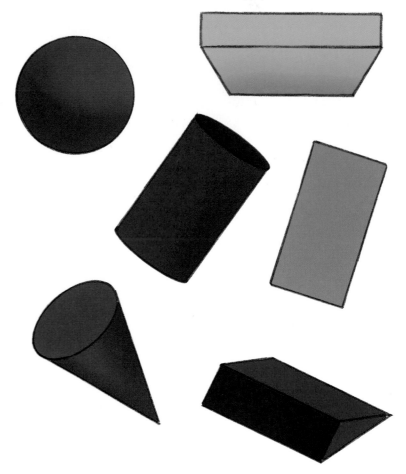

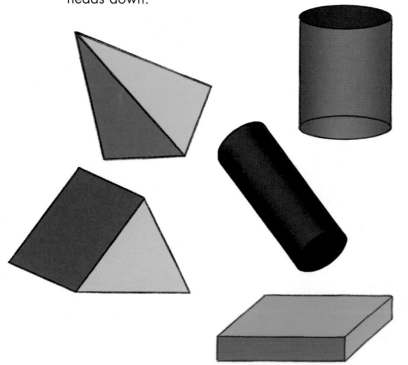

When you draw a manga character facing front, start with a matchstick drawing of the head (round), the neck and spine (straight verticals), the shoulders (slightly sloping horizontals), the hips (a short horizontal), and the arms and legs (long verticals).

At first it's the same for boys and girls. Then things get different. You need to draw a girl's chest as a downward-pointing triangle, with the bottom point touching the hips, also a downward-pointing triangle. Make the arms drop from the top points of the triangle. Draw a boy's upper chest first as an oval. Make the arms connect to it via small circles for the shoulder muscles.

There are other differences of course . . .

F R O N T V I E W

MALE

The basic pose . . .   is given shape . . .   some depth . . .   and is then fleshed out.

Girls have wider hips than boys and have more curves to their shape.

FEMALE

MALE

Note how the oval we drew for the boy's upper body has been squared off so that in the finished drawing he has a powerful, muscular chest.

FEMALE

You can see how the basic shapes drawn on to the matchstick figure determine the shape of the girl's finished body.

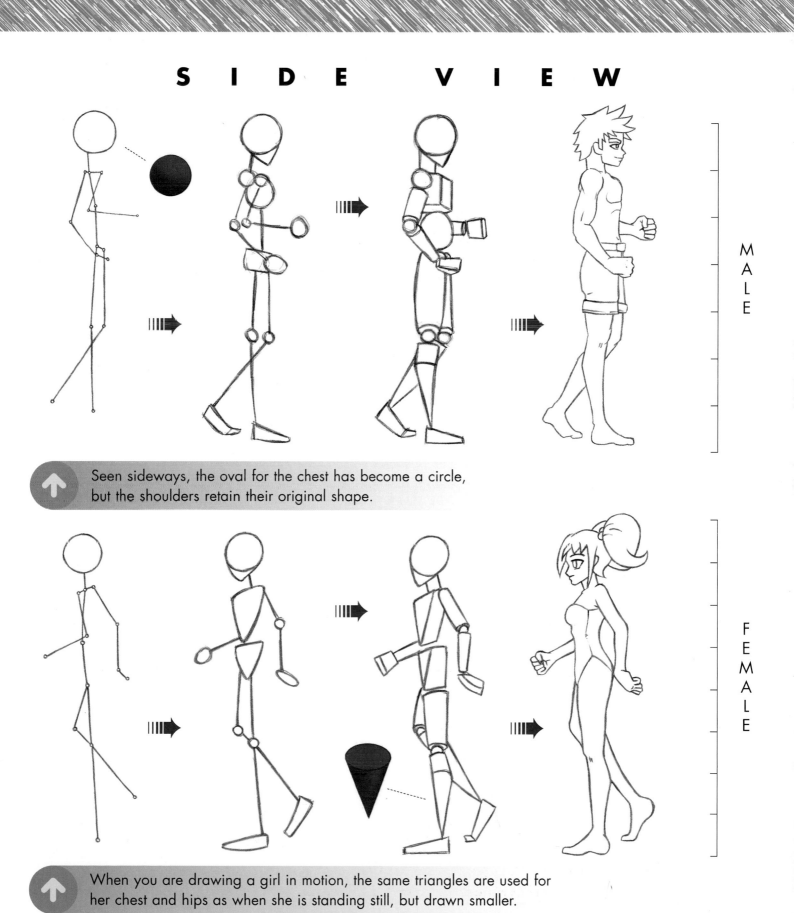

Seen sideways, the oval for the chest has become a circle, but the shoulders retain their original shape.

When you are drawing a girl in motion, the same triangles are used for her chest and hips as when she is standing still, but drawn smaller.

MALE

FEMALE

D-Boy

Age: 18

Location: Philadelphia, USA

Height: 6 ft 2 in

Weight: 210 lb

Interests, hobbies & skills: Basketball, hanging out with his crew, weight training.

D-Boy's the name: B-Ball's the game. D-Boy hasn't been called Daniel since he was a kid. Born and raised in Philly, he still lives there with his Mom and his Grandma.

He's a cool city boy through and through, but when it comes to basketball he's red hot. Even as a kid he was a 3-point master, and now he can sink it from halfcourt—no problem!

On the streets D-Boy wouldn't be caught dead without his cool shades and hot threads. Ice-cool, confident, and outgoing, no wonder he's leader of his crew.

Basketball is the A-Z of his life. When he's not leading his school team to a sweet victory, he's out playing 3-on-3 street ball, and when he's not ballin', he's working out in the gym.

On the streets and on the court, D-Boy's *The* Boy.

These rough drawings show D-Boy from different angles.

D-BOY

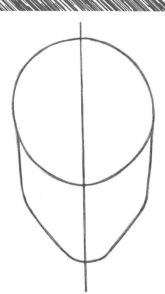

Step 1 →

Start D-Boy's head by sketching a circle with a vertical center line running through it. Now draw another two lines from either side of the circle, running parallel to the center line to start with, then gradually sloping toward each other before meeting.

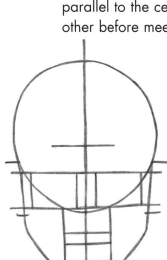

← **Step 2**

Sketch in two rectangles each side of the center line— they're gonna be the lenses of D-Boy's shades. Above and below on both sides, mark the top and bottom of his ears. Lightly draw three rectangles, one on top of the other to show where his nose and mouth will be.

Step 3 →

Now start to add the slanting eyebrows, shades, and lips. It's details like these that make D-Boy the one to watch.

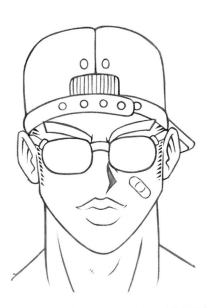

← **Step 4**

Add details to his cap and facial features. The lines on his neck suggest that the time spent in the gym hasn't been wasted. And dark sideburns give him the edge.

← **Step 5**

Bring the Boy to life by coloring his face and neck the flesh tone you think suits him best. Pencils? Ink? Paint? Use whatever you are most comfortable with, and make his eyebrows stand out by shading them quite dark.

Step 6 →

You can make D-Boy's face stand out from the page by adding shadows down one side. The darker shadow under his chin emphasizes the strong jawline.

EXPRESSIONS

Once you've mastered drawing D-Boy's head and face, you can start to have fun by varying his expression. Use the same basic steps to get his head and face on paper. But when you're adding the detail, vary the position of the eyebrows, the size and shape of his mouth, and the line of his jaw to show if he's freaking out or kicking back. When giving characters facial expressions, manga artists are less subtle than others. One look at the eyes, eyebrows, and mouth, and there is no doubt about the mood a manga character is in.

D-BOY

Starting with the head, draw the basic shapes that make up D-Boy's body—his chest, upper and lower arms, thighs, lower legs, and feet. And don't forget the ball, D-Boy's never without it. The head should fit into the body between five and six times.

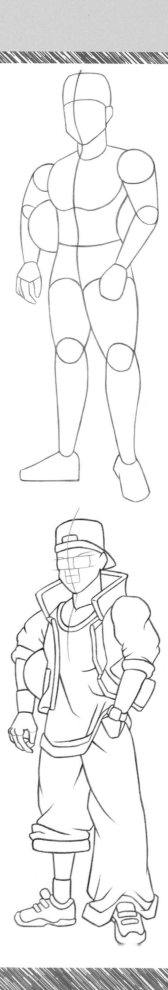

← **Step 2**

Now start to add D-Boy's cap, pants, and kicks, not forgetting that the right leg of his pants and the sleeves of his jacket are rolled up. When you've done that, you can erase some of the guidelines.

Step 3 →

The Boy's starting to look cool. He'll look even cooler when you draw in his wristwatch and the sweatband on his wrist, and the trim on his shoes. Show the way his clothes hang loosely on his body by adding one or two fold lines. Remember the small rectangles we used when we started to draw his face on page 16? Draw them in again.

Step 4

Put in his eyebrows, nose, and mouth. Sketch the band-aid on his left cheek and then add the stripes that run down his sleeves and pants. A little line on his chest, just above his shirt, shows D-Boy is big-time toned.

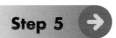

Step 5

It's time to get busy with the color pencils. You know how to color his face and shades. Use medium gray for the jacket and pants, with a lighter shade for the stripes, the trim of his kicks, and the number on his shirt; use a darker shade for the watchband and sweatband, shoes, and socks.

Step 6

Adding shadows down the right of his face and neck and to the folds of his clothes brings the Boy to life.

D-BOY

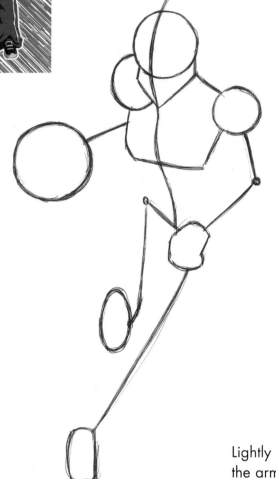

← **Step 1**

On court or on the street, D-Boy is always on the move. To capture this, begin by drawing a line of motion running from the top of his head, through the spine, and down the longer leg. Sketch in rough circles for his head, shoulders, hand, and, most important of all to D-Boy, the ball.

Step 2 →

Lightly draw in the basic shapes that suggest the arms, legs, and his free hand. Note how even at this stage, by making the D-Boy's right thigh broader but shorter than his left one, he seems to be jumping out of the page, ready to shoot.

DETAILS

The ball is all to D-Boy.

Watch it when D-Boy is on the move.

D-Boy's footgear is the buzz on the streets.

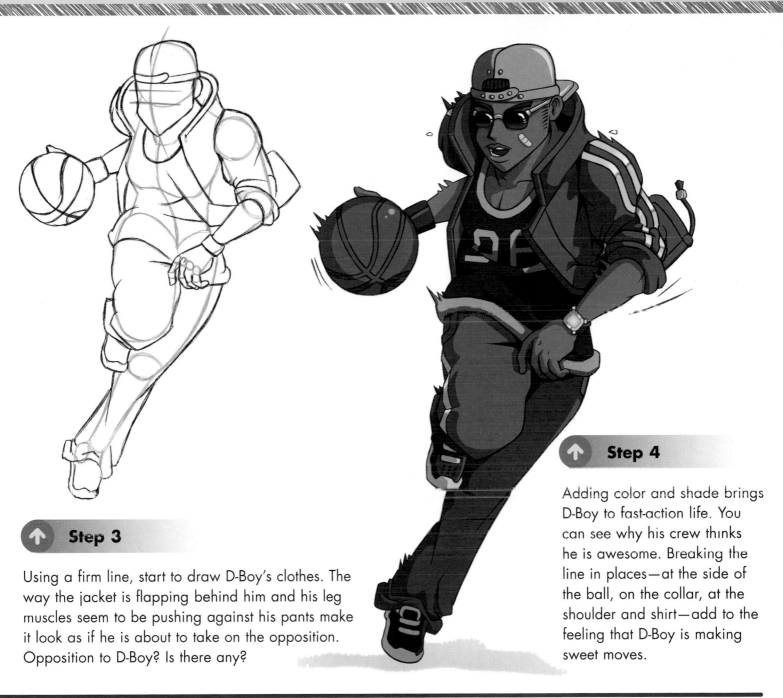

Step 3

Using a firm line, start to draw D-Boy's clothes. The way the jacket is flapping behind him and his leg muscles seem to be pushing against his pants make it look as if he is about to take on the opposition. Opposition to D-Boy? Is there any?

Step 4

Adding color and shade brings D-Boy to fast-action life. You can see why his crew thinks he is awesome. Breaking the line in places—at the side of the ball, on the collar, at the shoulder and shirt—add to the feeling that D-Boy is making sweet moves.

Super shades make a super guy super cool.

Getting the position of the thumb right is the key to drawing hands well.

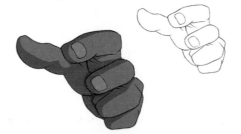

And to cap it all ....

Heather

Age: 17

Location: Tokyo, Japan

Height: 5 ft 6 in

Weight: 130 lb

Interests, hobbies & skills:
Technology, going to the gym,
& going to the movies.

How many teenagers live with a flame-throwing cat and have a robot for a houseboy? Heather does. Seventeen she may be, but sweet seventeen . . . ? She works out at the gym, she swims in the fast lane, and she's queen of the karate class.

Teflon-tough she may be, but she loves her diplomat dad and goes with him wherever he's based. Right now, that's in the bright lights of Tokyo. And that suits her just fine. It's great for the gizmos she buys whenever she can wheedle an advance on her allowance, and for the movies she loves. If it's a potential cult classic, she's first in line with her friends to buy a ticket. She's into fast action, horror, and sci-fi—the faster the action, the more horrible the horror, and the more 'sci' the 'fi,' the better.

She's got friends in places from Milan, Italy to Oahu, Hawaii. Luckily for Dad, she spends as much time on her school work as she does on the internet catching up with her pals, and is a grade-A student.

These rough drawings show off Heather's cute, cheeky side.

HEATHER

Step 1

If it helps, think of the two basic shapes that make up the face and chin as an egg. Keep practicing: it won't be long before the first stage of drawing any face comes as easily to you as chewing gum. The line of axis that we are going to draw Heather's face on is angled to one side a little.

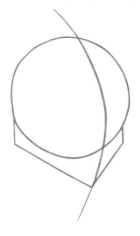

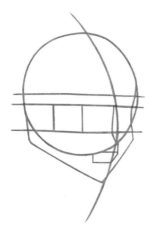

Step 2

Draw in the eye-level line and start on the preliminary details. Looking to one side, the eye further away is going to be smaller and a bit narrower than the nearer one. Remember this when you begin to work on the eyes and eyebrows. And remember that manga girls' eyes are always larger than boys'. The girls have longer eyelashes, too. The direction of the eyes will depend on what is catching Heather's eye at any given moment.

Step 3

If you have trouble drawing characters looking to one side, try holding the paper up to the light and looking at it from behind. This often helps to see where you've gone wrong.

Step 4

When the basic details have been completed, you can start to ink in the lines. To get Heather's thick, dark eyelashes, use black India ink and a brush pen. Her hair should look as if it is growing out of her head (like the real thing) and not added as an afterthought.

Step 5

You can see the different shapes of the eyes quite clearly here, now that we have applied flat color to the finished black ink drawing. Make sure the pupils are fixed on the same point. If they are not, you won't be able to tell where Heather is looking. And note that her nose is little more than a tiny black triangle.

Step 6

There are several different types of shading when it comes to highlighting eyes. Here the result is to give those giant orbs sparkle and luster. For the hair, highlight the area where it catches the light.

EXPRESSIONS

Understandably, Heather gets upset whenever she has to move and leave all her friends behind. With her downcast eyes, downturned mouth, and furrowed eyebrows, it is easy to see how sad she is. And just to make sure that there is no doubt as to the mood she's in, the mascara running down from both eyes is a telling detail. But Heather's never sad for long. With eyebrows raised, eyes wide open, pupils shining, and her mouth open in a delightful smile, it's plain to see that Heather is the happiest girl in the world!

HEATHER

Step 1

You get a good idea of the basic body proportions from this preliminary sketch of Heather, hand on hip, in what's going to be a typically aggressive pose. Note that the elbow joint is just above the hip bone and about level with the waist.

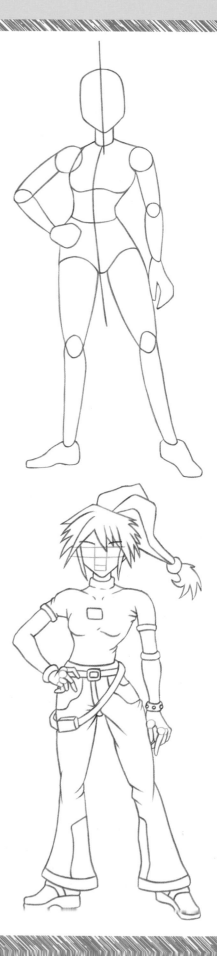

Step 2

The arm length should be about 2.5 times the height of her head, and the wrist about level with her thigh when the arm is straight along the side of the body. Two soft curves on the body at about halfway down the upper arm suggest Heather's trim, firm figure. When you are happy that no more corrections are needed, apart from erasing some of the guidelines, start inking in the outline and some of the detail on her clothing.

Step 3

Hands are probably the hardest thing to draw; even experienced artists can have trouble getting them exactly right—ever wondered why Mickey Mouse wears gloves? We've concentrated on getting them right, along with Heather's clothes and body, before starting to work on her eyes and mouth. She's going to be staring straight ahead, so both eyes should be the same size and symmetrical.

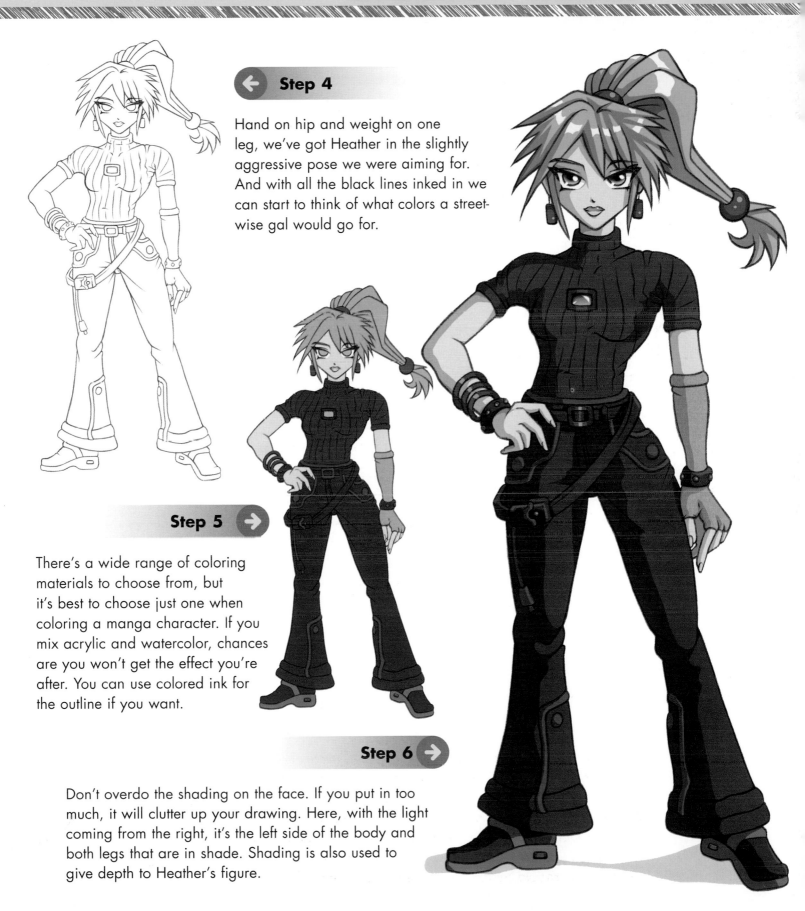

Step 4

Hand on hip and weight on one leg, we've got Heather in the slightly aggressive pose we were aiming for. And with all the black lines inked in we can start to think of what colors a streetwise gal would go for.

Step 5

There's a wide range of coloring materials to choose from, but it's best to choose just one when coloring a manga character. If you mix acrylic and watercolor, chances are you won't get the effect you're after. You can use colored ink for the outline if you want.

Step 6

Don't overdo the shading on the face. If you put in too much, it will clutter up your drawing. Here, with the light coming from the right, it's the left side of the body and both legs that are in shade. Shading is also used to give depth to Heather's figure.

HEATHER

Step 1

The preliminary matchstick figure not only helps you establish the position, it also ensures that you have all the proportions just right before moving on to the next step. The length of a fully stretched leg should be about half the total height of the body. It's easy at this stage to make any corrections necessary to get the pose you want.

Step 2

Manga girls have narrow waists and wide hips. You may not be able to see this in the final drawing, but don't be tempted to make shortcuts. Even the most experienced manga artists take care with each step, not progressing to the next step until they are 100 per cent satisfied with the one they've been working on.

DETAILS

The girl gets a great kick out of her shoes.

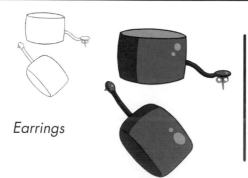

Earrings

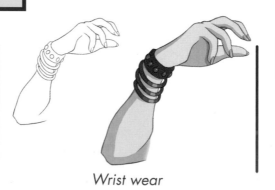

Wrist wear

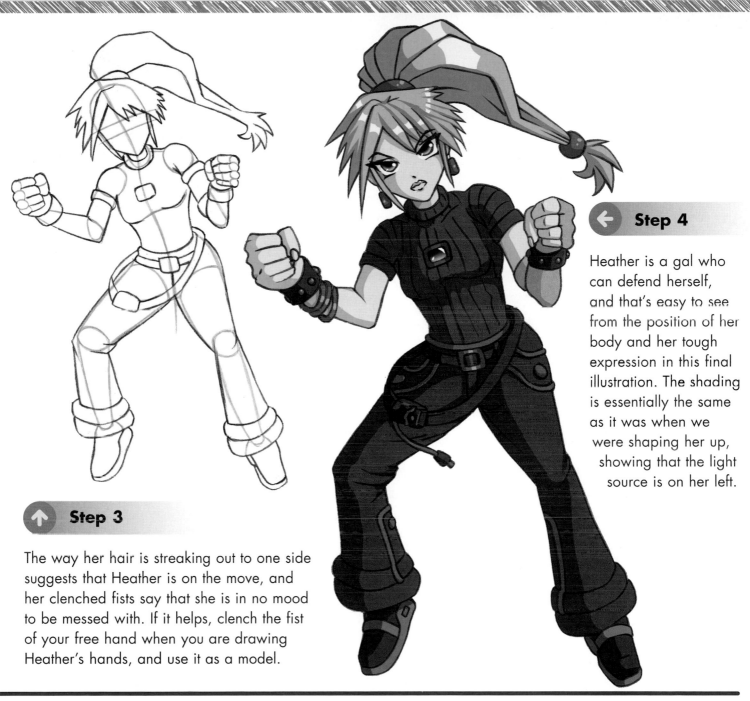

Step 4

Heather is a gal who can defend herself, and that's easy to see from the position of her body and her tough expression in this final illustration. The shading is essentially the same as it was when we were shaping her up, showing that the light source is on her left.

Step 3

The way her hair is streaking out to one side suggests that Heather is on the move, and her clenched fists say that she is in no mood to be messed with. If it helps, clench the fist of your free hand when you are drawing Heather's hands, and use it as a model.

Little details, like her bangles and nail polish, are a nice contrast to her tough appearance.

Her belt is always worn loose.

A long, fingerless glove on one arm is a great individual touch.

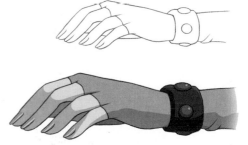

J.C.

Age: 15

Location: London, England

Height: 5 ft 10 in

Weight: 140 lb

Interests, hobbies & skills: Playing guitar, singing in his band, and writing music.

J.C. is fifteen. He longs to be famous. He envisions gigs crammed with screaming girls, and boys spiking their hair to be like him. In reality he's a boy from London, who plays locally and has to do his homework, like everyone else.

His mum and dad are quietly amused by his dream but very supportive. They want him to be happy and get to the top—in whatever career he chooses. They know he has a heart of gold and that success would not spoil him.

J.C. lives music. He breathes music. When he's not performing, he's running riffs on his guitar, and when he's not stroking the strings, chances are he's writing another new song. Or maybe he's standing in front of a mirror, coaxing his hair into even sharper spikes.

When J.C.'s not trying to get his career off the ground, he hangs out with his friends. At the end of a tiring session, J.C. and his band will invite their friends around to share a pizza while they chill out and watch MTV. His best friend is Kimi, the girl you'll meet next. J.C. and Kimi go back—and, with the internet, the fact that she now lives in Canada, is no problem. She is the first one he'll let listen to a new song. She is his Number One fan!

But J.C. is so focused on getting to the top he'll never relax for long. After an hour he'll feel the need to get out his guitar, run some riffs and shout, 'OK guys! Let's rrrock!'

These roughs show J.C. trying out poses for his future album cover!

J.C.

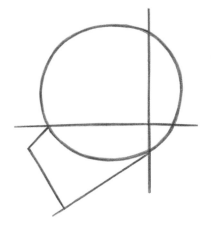

Draw a circle first, then a cross with the vertical near the right side and the horizontal close to the bottom. Add part of a rough rectangle shape from where the two lines leave the circle at the left and bottom.

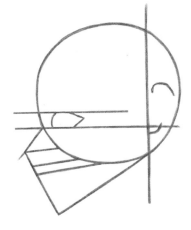

← **Step 2**

The top corner of the rectangle is going to be the tip of J.C.'s nose; the bottom corner, his jaw. Draw two lines to show where his mouth will be. The bottom of his eye is on the horizontal line, and the top of his ear is in the section of the circle that's to the right of the vertical line.

Step 3 →

Pressing harder on your pencil, firm up the lines of J.C.'s lower profile—his nose, lips, chin, and jaw. Lightly sketch in his ear—an ear for music if ever there was one. Now get going on the hair—the spikes that every would-be rock kid wants.

← **Step 4**

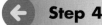

Firm up the lines and add some detail to his spiky hair. The guidelines can go now: they've done their job. Draw in his eyeball, remembering that eyes are the most pronounced features of manga characters. And don't forget the beads and earring. J.C. never does.

Step 5

When you're coloring in the skin, remember that aspiring rock stars don't see a lot of daylight. That shock of hair is a rich copper color, complemented by the silver beads around his neck.

Step 6

Dark shading down the left side of the spikes makes each one stand out like the Easter Bunny on Christmas Day. Finish with lighter shading down the profile and neck. In six short steps, you've turned a circle and a bit of a rectangle into one cool character. Rock on!

EXPRESSIONS

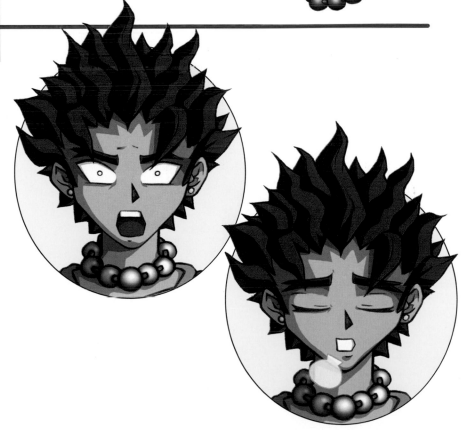

When you're giving a guy expression, it's usually the mouth, eyes, and eyebrows that change to suit the mood: a nose is a nose is a nose, after all—there's not much you can do with it. In the top picture, with his eyes wide open, the pupils little more than pinpricks, J.C. is obviously surprised about something. This is emphasized by his open mouth. In the lower picture, the rocker's eyes are just slightly curved slits beneath his brows and his mouth has become a little square. These subtle changes now show that he is relieved.

J.C.

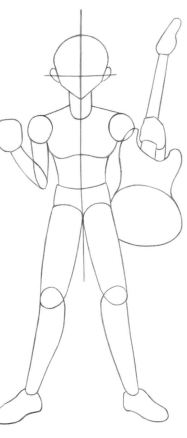

Step 1

We're going to draw a front view of J.C. Start with two intersecting guidelines, then draw in the basic shapes that make up the rocker's torso, limbs, and guitar. The main body-shapes form part of a rough triangle, curving down toward the stomach.

Step 2

Start to sketch in the ripped T-shirt (J.C. rips his clothes to give them a cool, cutting edge!) and flared jeans. Sketch in the famous spikes. Add the hands as clenched fists to suggest the power J.C. generates when he's on stage.

Step 3

Time to start adding some detail—creases and fold-lines on J.C's clothes, laces on his shoes, and details on his face. Manga noses are simple wedges, and the mouths are usually quite small. The eyes should be a little more than one eye-width apart.

SHAPING UP

← **Step 4**

Now that J.C. is looking like the budding star he is, you can give him more definition. When you're drawing in the final details, press harder with your pencil to make a strong, firm line.

Step 5 →

Color gives a character, erm . . . character! J.C. likes his clothes to be as cool as he is himself. A dull orange for the T-shirt and a sludgy, muddy color for his jeans give him the grunge look he likes. His matching rings and beads add to his style.

Step 6 →

Shading can be a bit tricky at first, but it's worth hanging in there and getting it right. Think of J.C. standing in the spotlight he loves so much and think which part of him will be brighter than the rest. Add shading to the fold lines to flesh out his clothes.

J.C.

← **Step 1**

Now we're drawing J.C. in profile doing what he likes doing best—performing. Start with a guideline that shows the kneeling position he's in, then draw in the basic circles, rectangles, and triangles that make up his head, hands, shoulders, upper body, and feet.

Step 2 →

Work around the guideline and basic shapes to flesh out the skeleton. Keep it very simple: if you try to put in any detail at this stage, chances are that you'll have to use an eraser later! We want to be sure that we draw the kneeling position just right.

DETAILS

Beads can give a kid character.

Sweatbands break the solid line of the lower arm.

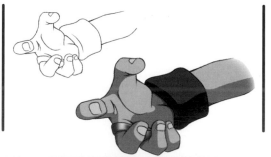

The triangles you drew for J.C.'s feet fit into his shoes.

Step 4

Draw his eyes as slits to show how hard he is concentrating on his music. His mouth should be a triangular 'u' shape. By keeping it simple in the beginning steps and making sure the position is just right, you've really got J.C. rocking.

Step 3

Even kneeling, the basic proportions are the same—upper arm just less than one head height, wrist to elbow just a bit longer. The knee should be two head heights above the bottom of the foot. Start adding the details once you're satisfied that you have it right.

Most hands start as rectangles joined together.

Don't forget his guitar!

Next time you're perfecting a parallel, and a bundle of blue blasts past positively pulverizing the powder, it's a sure bet that it's Kimi—she's all speed on a snowboard. Like all her girlfriends—and she's got plenty—she'll shop till she drops, especially if there's a dance to go to and she has simply nothing to wear! But her heart belongs to the slopes. Her family have just moved to Canada and Kimi's taken to life there like a duck to water. Heli-skiing, white-water rafting, hang-gliding: Kimi loves them all; the more dangerous the better. But snowboarding is what she does best.

She jets to slopes all over the world whenever she can, winning so many competitions that the shelves in her room groan under the weight of the cups and trophies she's scooped. The walls are covered in pics of her favorite places and favorite friends. Somewhere among them is a long list of the countries she's going to return to when she's on the around-the-world trip she's promised herself after college. Until then, she's happy to grab her board, whoop, 'Time to shred the slope!,' and head for the chairlift.

Kimi

Age: 16

Location: Vancouver, Canada

Height: 5 ft 4 in

Weight: 120 lb

Interests, hobbies & skills: Snowboarding, hanging out with friends, and traveling.

You can see in this rough that Kimi's eyes light up when she thinks of snowboarding!

KIMI

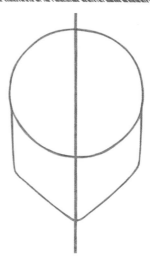

All manga girls, even a fit snowboarder like Kimi, have faces that are smaller and rounder than the guys. The angles are softer and less sharp, too. Keep this in mind when you're drawing a circle for Kimi's head, and the sloping lines that make up her jaw. Don't forget the center line.

Step 2

Use the center line to make sure that the shapes on the left mirror the ones on the right. Remember that manga girls' eyes are bigger and wider than the males of the species.

Step 3

Use the rectangles below the circle to position Kimi's mouth. Draw two small, upward-curving lines for her upper lip, and a single smaller, downward curve for her lower one. A small tick shape from where the center line crosses the bottom of the circle to above the upper lip indicates her nose.

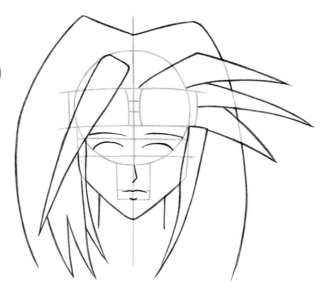

Step 4

Start on the detail, including the hair—a striking feature of all manga characters. Getting it right isn't easy, but think of each tress as a stretched-out triangle and you'll soon get the hang of it. Note how some hair flops over the goggles Kimi uses to keep it in place. Her thick, dark eyelashes are going to help to make her shining eyes even more striking.

A light skin tone and shades of blue and purple capture Kimi's cool good looks; no wonder she's as popular off the slopes as she is on them. Darkening the line around each lock of her hair emphasizes its thickness. Her cute nose is basically two little tick marks, but even at this stage, it looks 3-D.

Step 6

The technical term for the white reflection in Kimi's eyes and on her goggles is a 'specular'. Speculars show where the light is coming from. Light purple streaks make her hair glow.

EXPRESSIONS

A raised eyebrow, a simple change to the mouth and the position of her eyeballs, and Kimi looks as if she's in questioning mood (near right). To make her seem upset (far right) we have angled the eyebrows, opened her mouth and made it a downward-curving lozenge shape, with a tiny shaded line at either side. Raised cheekbones are suggested by a downward curve under each eye. With these alterations and the white, glistening tears, the artist has made it clear that the normally bubbly Kimi is sad about something. Experiment with changes like these to give your manga characters different expressions.

KIMI

Step 1

Here, Kimi is not quite fully facing front, so the vertical is slightly off-center. The principle stays the same. Break the body into basic shapes, taking into account the position of Kimi's arms—one bent to balance her snowboard, the other on her hip.

Step 2

Kimi's pants are loose to allow for her boots. Draw in the outline of Kimi's snowboard—which is essentially a rectangle that curves a little—and her ski boots. She's starting to look ready for action.

Step 3

Add some lines to suggest the way Kimi's ski gear fits her body and moves with it. Give the board some depth by drawing a second line down the left side, following the curve of the first one. Now do more work on her face, noting that she's going to be smiling, and that the rectangles differ in size side to side of the 'center line.'

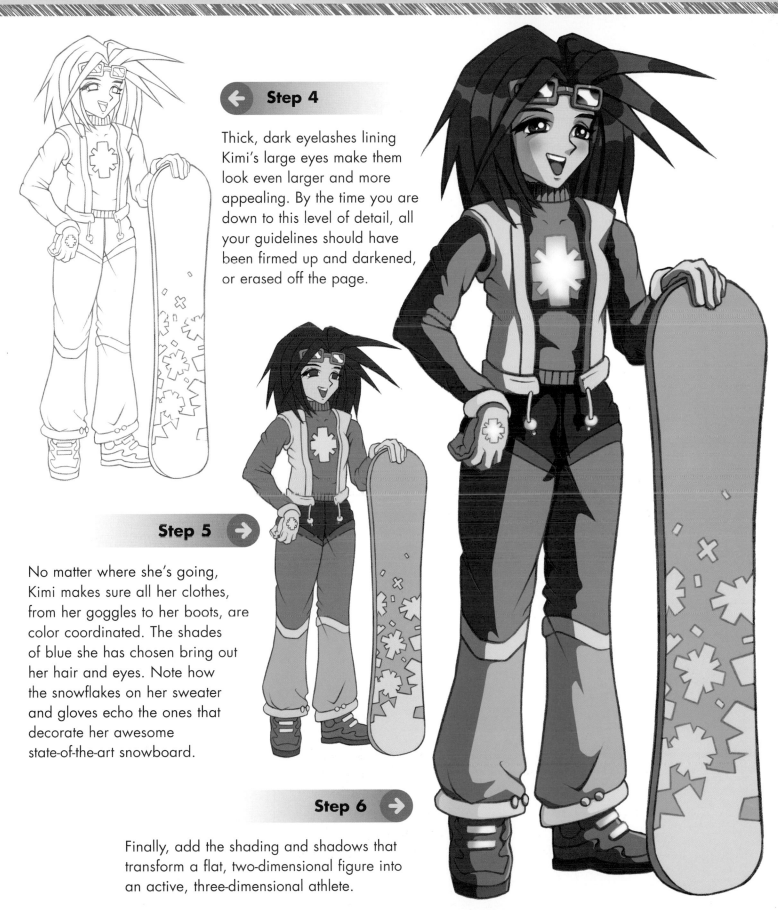

Step 4 ←

Thick, dark eyelashes lining Kimi's large eyes make them look even larger and more appealing. By the time you are down to this level of detail, all your guidelines should have been firmed up and darkened, or erased off the page.

Step 5 →

No matter where she's going, Kimi makes sure all her clothes, from her goggles to her boots, are color coordinated. The shades of blue she has chosen bring out her hair and eyes. Note how the snowflakes on her sweater and gloves echo the ones that decorate her awesome state-of-the-art snowboard.

Step 6 →

Finally, add the shading and shadows that transform a flat, two-dimensional figure into an active, three-dimensional athlete.

KIMI

← **Step 1**

Draw the guidelines for Kimi's arms and legs as well as the basic shapes that make up her body. Don't forget to add dots for joints.

Step 2 →

Next time you see a picture of a sports star in action, study it carefully, trying to imagine the basic skeleton beneath the flesh. That will help you to build up your matchstick figure. Note the angle of the body: here it's turned a bit to one side, which is why we've drawn the line of motion a bit off-center.

DETAILS

Goggles are cool off the slopes and on.

Kimi knows that gloves don't have to be dull.

Boots are molded to ensure a perfect fit.

Step 3

A lot of budding manga artists make the mistake of trying to move too quickly from one step to the next. Don't fall into that trap. Only when you're sure you have it right should you start to get Kimi into her boarding gear and add the hair streaming out behind her, suggesting movement—fast movement!

Step 4

With a smile on her face and her eyes sparkling, Kimi is on a real up. If you look at the first step, you can see that it would have been impossible to capture Kimi in full action like this, if we hadn't spent time getting her pose just right. Now she looks exactly what she is—THE Snow Queen.

Kimi's most precious possession.

Studying your own hand can help a lot.

STRIKER

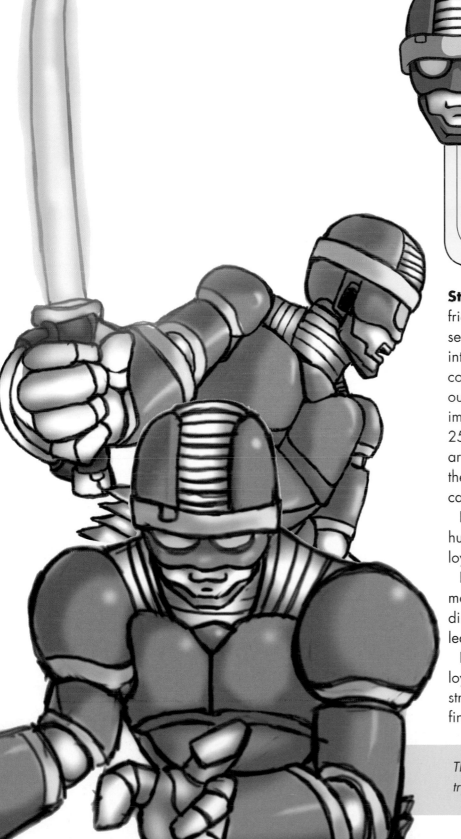

Striker

Age: 2

Location: Tokyo, Japan

Height: 6 ft 4 in

Weight: 250 lb

Interests, hobbies & skills:
Incredible strength, multilingual,
keeps a very clean and tidy house!

Striker came into Heather's life when a friend of her dad's was working on a top-secret Artificial Intelligence project. He was intended to be an assault machine, but courtesy of a computer malfunction, he turned out to be a domestic treasure. Standing an impressive 6 ft 4 in tall and weighing in at 250 lb, Striker cuts quite a figure as he stomps around the house—dusting here and polishing there, washing the dishes one minute and the car the next.

But Heather and Striker are more than human and domestic servant—they are also loyal friends to each other.

Heather's friends are impressed and their mothers often cast an envious eye in Striker's direction, but there's no way he would ever leave Heather. Where she goes, he'll go, too.

But it's not just in the housework and loyalty departments that Striker has his strengths. He can lift Heather with just one finger. How strong is that?

These roughs are a great way to try Striker in different poses.

STRIKER

We're going to draw Striker, left shoulder closer to us and his head turning to glance behind him. He has a large head and a strong jawline. Start by drawing what looks a bit like a teacup seen from above!

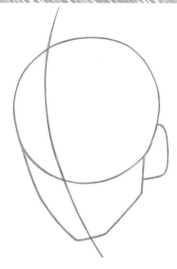

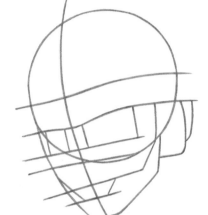

Step 2

His left eye is going to be closer to us than his right, so it will be larger. Draw it to the right of the 'central' line running down the left of his face. The vertical band sloping across his brow connects his CPU, which is removable, to his face.

Step 3

Striker's mouth sits in the middle of a strip of soft metal fabric beneath his eyes. Once you've sketched these in, and the ears (aural detectors in A-I speak) on either side of his head, you can ink in the main outline and some of the detail, keeping some of the original guidelines to help you with the next stage.

Step 4

At the end of this step, Striker should look as if he has been in a bad accident, with the top of his head and his neck swathed in bandages. That's what happens when you're made of metal! Make sure your pencil lines here are more or less parallel before inking them in. If they're not, Striker will look like a distinctly unhappy robot.

 Step 5

Striker may look like an artificial insect, with his large, deep blue eyes gazing out from beneath his helmet-like head, but he has an air of intelligence and humanity about him. There are no set rules about coloring in manga metal robots. Let's color him a muddy camouflage color since he was originally intended to be a fighting machine.

Step 6

The metallic Striker gleams when he's caught in the light. That is why we highlighted parts of his head, neck, and back. We've also put in a little shading down the side.

EXPRESSIONS

In manga, a robot's face can be as expressive as any other character. In the first image, the open mouth with bared 'teeth' and glaring red eyes show us that Striker is in a fury. In the next picture, spirals in the eyes and the downturned open mouth suggest that Heather's loyal friend has been made dizzy with surprise. (Either that or he is watching the spin cycle of a washer!) Experiment with different drawing devices and see how many other expressions you can give him. Try narrowing his eyes or puckering his mouth.

STRIKER

 Step 1

Striker's basic proportions are almost the same as those of manga humans. His arms are slightly longer; the tips of his digits reaching to almost halfway down his thigh. Before you move on, make sure your basic figure looks strong and powerful. Don't overdo it— he's lean and was meant to be mean.

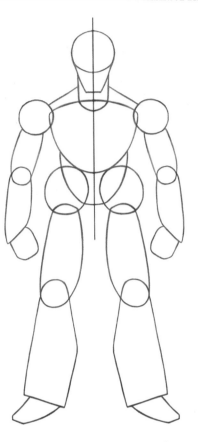

Step 2

Note how overlapping areas in the basic shapes in Striker's arms and legs have become the elbow and knee joints. And as we draw the full robot, his body on the right side of the central axis is a mirror image of the left side.

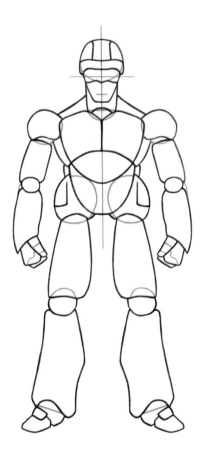

Step 3

Have you noticed the quite intricate robot hands? Clenched or open, both look strong enough to crush a metal bar to mush. Details like this give your manga creations character.

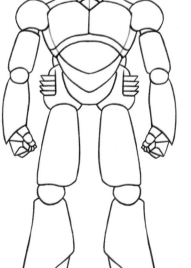

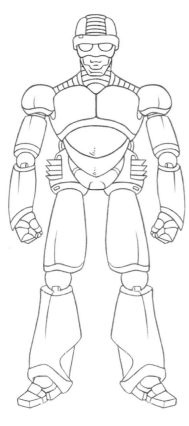

Step 4

When the detail is complete and all the pencil lines have been inked over, Striker looks as if he has stepped straight out of a black-and-white sci-fi movie. There is still time to work on the final detail like the grilles at his hips.

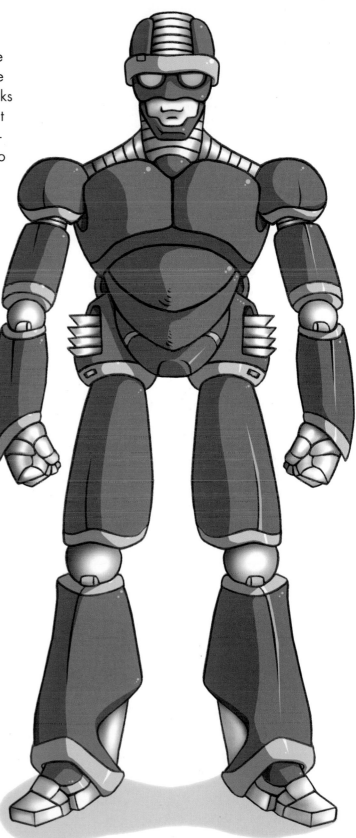

Step 5

Marker pens are great for applying large areas of color, like the brown we've used here. For the best effect, work carefully in the same direction, taking care not to smudge over the black outline. Use a brush pen for the detail, again working carefully.

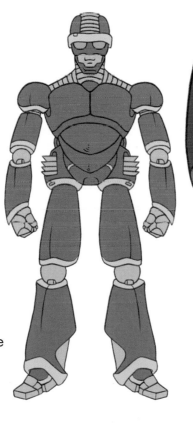

Step 6

With the light coming from the right, Striker's left side is strongly shaded. The white highlights on the joints and other light metal-colored parts make Striker a glow-rious A-I machine!

STRIKER

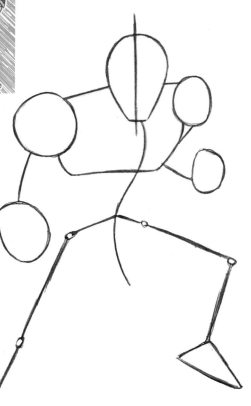

← **Step 1**

Take a minute or two to study the finished picture of Striker on the next page and try to see how his weight is distributed. Notice how we can see only his upper right arm and that the parts of his body nearest to us appear larger than those further away. Reflect all this in your preliminary sketch of the A-I machine.

Step 2 →

Outline Striker's massive legs and arms around Step 1's matchstick figure. His huge right fist blocks our view of his lower arm. And because of his pose, we can see more of one side of his upper body than the other. That's why we drew the central axis line to one side.

DETAILS

Side vents help Striker to keep his cool.

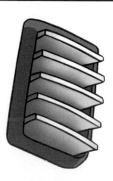

Beware of telling Striker to get a grip.

Fantastic 'feet' of engineering!

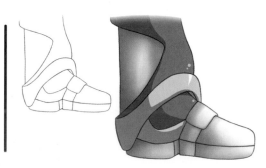

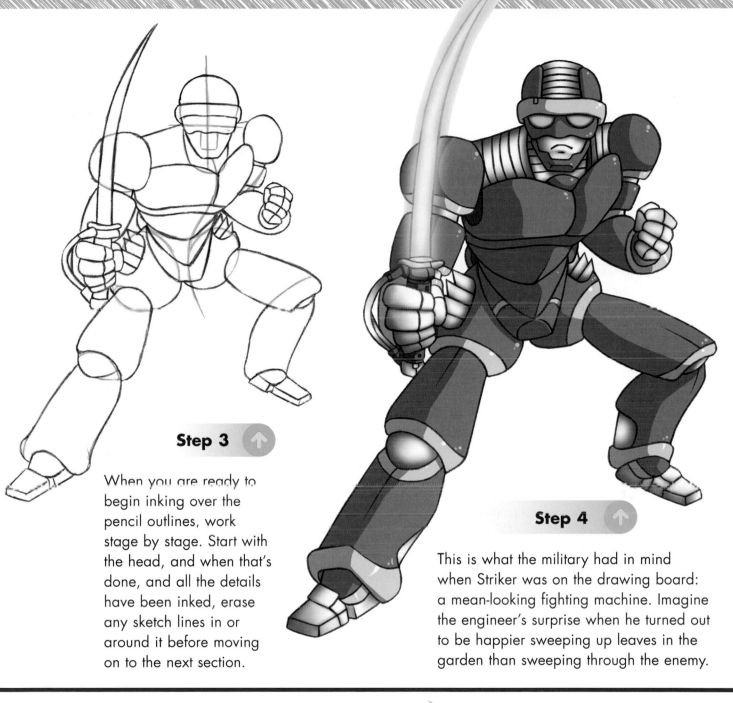

Step 3

When you are ready to begin inking over the pencil outlines, work stage by stage. Start with the head, and when that's done, and all the details have been inked, erase any sketch lines in or around it before moving on to the next section.

Step 4

This is what the military had in mind when Striker was on the drawing board: a mean-looking fighting machine. Imagine the engineer's surprise when he turned out to be happier sweeping up leaves in the garden than sweeping through the enemy.

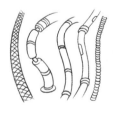

Wired for action.

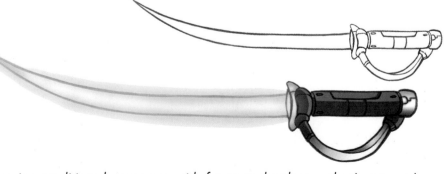

Marrying traditional weapons with future technology—that's manga!

Kit-Kit

Age: 4

Location: Tokyo, Japan

Height: 3 ft 6 in

Weight: 190 lb

Interests, hobbies & skills:
Breathes fire and is fire resistant, has the ability to turn invisible.

Who's the coolest cat in the neighborhood? Who's got a tail that burns brighter than a Fourth of July firework? Who can do a very cool vanishing act when necessary: here one moment, gone the next? And who uses that talent to stir up a little trouble (OK, a lot)? Kit-Kit, Heather's favorite feline, that's who.

Sure, he has his faults. He sleeps a lot, he eats a lot. And he's not too fussy about whose food he gets his whiskers into. When Kit-Kit gets nervous and his tail goes into flame-throwing mode, everyone knows he's been up to no good.

Despite his faults, he is immensely kind and considerate. He is a loyal friend and would sacrifice himself, if necessary, to defend Heather. Luckily, Kit-Kit has nine lives—how awesome is that?

Kit-Kit is at his most relaxed in these rough drawings.

KIT-KIT

Step 1

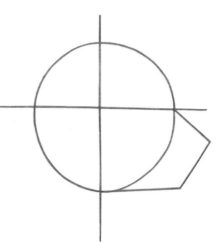

All cats, even funky felines like Kit-Kit, have pointed snouts that slope down from above the eyes. Begin in the usual way—a circle, with a cross running through it. Add a sawn-off triangle shape sticking out from the circumference at the bottom-right.

Step 2

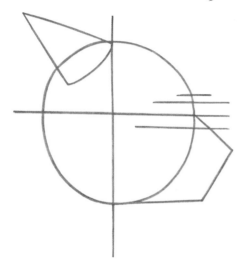

Eyes are big in manga art—especially when drawing animals. It's vital to get the position right or K-K is going to be one very uncool cat. Two horizontal lines—one above and one below the center line—indicate where the eyes will be. The cone shape opposite the snout will eventually become the ear.

Step 3

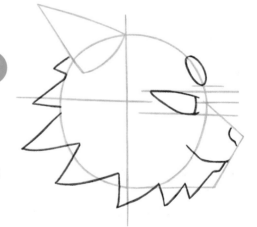

The outline of an almond-shaped slanting eye, the beginnings of his mouth, the suggestion of a nose, the start of a ruff of fur around the neck and K-K is starting to look like the real thing. Even at this stage there's just a hint of mischief about him.

Step 4

Manga animals' eyebrows are just as important to their finished look and expressions as they are to other members of the manga clan. Starting from the middle of the brow, K-K's eyebrows sweep back elegantly toward his pointed ear, which balances his snout. The tooth sticking out the side of his mouth suggests that this cat may be a pampered pet, but deep down he's a hunter!

← Step 5

Even manga animals have the trademark manga hair. You can make it any color you like, but make sure it's darker than the rest of K-K's face and neck, so it will add to our understanding of his character. Use a bright red as the base color for his eyes to suggest that they burn as brightly as his flaming tail.

Step 6 →

A mighty mane. Glittering eyes. An alert look on his face. Don't worry if your first attempt looks more like a dog's dinner than a crazy cat. Drawing manga animal faces is far from easy. But it's worth staying with it.

EXPRESSIONS

If you have a cat of your own, you know that it has a wide range of expressions, just like a person. In the picture on the near right, Kit-Kit's open mouth and the position of his pupils show what is on his mind. The bared teeth and gleaming eyes show that he is as alert as a panther on the prowl. He looks as if he is about to pounce on something—perhaps a mouse? In the next image, we see him in a different state. The closed eyes are indicated by the black, upward-sloping curves, and his mouth is slightly open. He is the picture of total contentment as he enjoys a well-earned snooze.

KIT-KIT

Step 1

Now we will draw Kit-Kit's head not quite fully facing us. There will be the same space on either side of the horizontal line in the triangle that will become that magnificent manga head. At this stage, the body and limbs are just fifteen simple, connecting shapes.

Step 2

One of Kit-Kit's paws is going to be in shadow, so you won't have to do much more than giving it a little shape and fur. Work on the other three legs. They may look clumsy, but like all cats, K-K can prowl around Heather's house as quietly as a mouse!

Step 3

Start to add tufts of fur on the tail and legs, and draw in a little detail to the ears. By the end of this stage you should have the outline of one cool cat. His pose suggests the power and agility common to all cats in top condition. And if there is one cat who's at that top, it's K-K.

Step 4 →

The eyebrows rising sharply from the crest on his brow and the two sharp little teeth protruding from his mouth remind us that K-K is a close cousin of the big cats that live in the wild. Two things they don't have though: a manga mark on their hindquarters and a blazing tail.

← Step 5

We've colored his body a soft pastel; you can choose whatever color you think suits him best. Match his mane to his manga mark: he is as proud of one as he is of the other. At this stage, K-K looks as if he could be about to fade from the scene for a while—something he does whenever he's in trouble.

Step 6 →

Outlined in red and with a white-hot center, you can almost feel the heat from K-K's flaming tail. The sharp eyes, focused on something—food probably—glow from his face. As he is standing on all fours, don't forget to add some shadow around the area he's standing in. And shading the back, off-side leg quite dark gives him the 3-D quality you're after.

KIT-KIT

When you are drawing K-K in an action pose, try one that is dramatic, or even scary. The body is going to be foreshortened, so a simple circle will do for now. Put the center line to one side of the head shape. Draw matchstick legs with dots for the joints.

Step 2

The drawing at the end of this stage should capture the basic pose of a cat on the alert and ready to pounce. You can see how the short, back-right leg is starting to give K-K the depth you are aiming for in the final picture. Fleshed out only a little like this, he could almost be mistaken for some kind of animal-droid from a sci-fi movie.

DETAILS

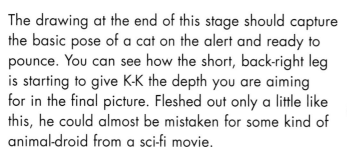

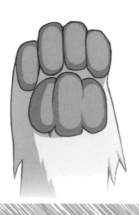

Soft pads help Kit prowl noiselessly.

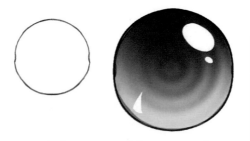

Leave little areas of the crest white to show how it shines.

Sharp claws for a sharp cat.

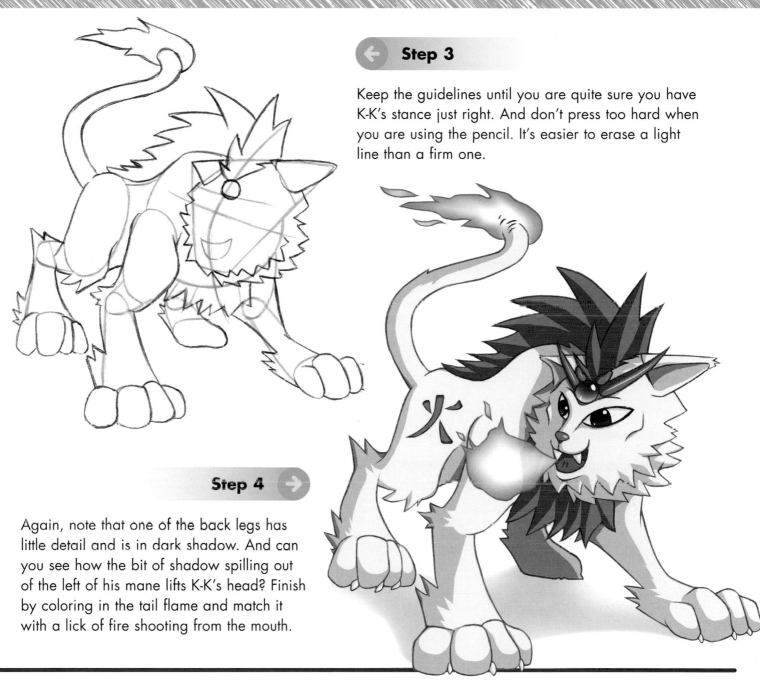

Step 3

Keep the guidelines until you are quite sure you have K-K's stance just right. And don't press too hard when you are using the pencil. It's easier to erase a light line than a firm one.

Step 4

Again, note that one of the back legs has little detail and is in dark shadow. And can you see how the bit of shadow spilling out of the left of his mane lifts K-K's head? Finish by coloring in the tail flame and match it with a lick of fire shooting from the mouth.

'Other cats, keep off!'

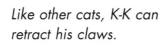

Like other cats, K-K can retract his claws.

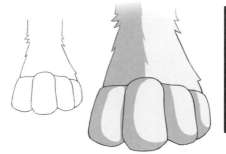

Sometimes K-K gets all fired up.

START CREATING YOUR OWN CHARACTERS NOW THAT YOU'VE MASTERED OURS.
DON'T WORRY IF YOU DON'T GET THEM RIGHT FIRST TIME. KEEP REVISTING THE LESSONS YOU
HAVE LEARNED IN THIS BOOK AND YOU WILL SOON DEVELOP A STYLE ALL OF YOUR OWN.

GOOD LUCK AND HAVE FUN!